MY LIFE AS A
HINDU

FLEUR BRADLEY

45TH PARALLEL PRESS

Published in the United States of America by Cherry Lake Publishing Group
Ann Arbor, Michigan
www.cherrylakepublishing.com

Editorial Consultant: Dr. Virginia Loh-Hagan, EdD, Literacy, San Diego State University
Content Adviser: Molly H. Bassett, Associate Professor and Chair in the Department of Religious Studies
    at Georgia State University
Reading Adviser: Beth Walker Gambro, MS, Ed., Reading Consultant, Yorkville, IL
Book Designer: Jen Wahi

Photo Credits: © StockByM/istock, cover, 1; © sunsetman/Shutterstock, 4; Public Domain/Wikimedia, 7;
    © Clovera/Shutterstock, 8; © Gauri Nigudkar/Shutterstock, 12; © Martial Red/Shutterstock, 14; © RAMNIKLAL
    MODI/Shutterstock, 15; © gorkhe1980/Shutterstock, 17; © Shyamalamuralinath/Shutterstock, 18; © Chaitali
    Mitra/Shutterstock, 23; © Vijay Sundararaman Iyer/Wikimedia, 24; © Prabhjit S. Kalsi/Shutterstock, 28;
    © Sukhvinder Saggu/Shutterstock, 29; © LAKSHI CREATIVE BUSINESS/Shutterstock, 30

45th Parallel Press is an imprint of Cherry Lake Publishing Group.

Library of Congress Cataloging-in-Publication Data

Names: Bradley, Fleur, author.
Title: My life as a Hindu / by Fleur Bradley.
Description: Ann Arbor : Cherry Lake Publishing, 2022. | Series: How the world worships
Identifiers: LCCN 2021039874 | ISBN 9781534199415 (hardcover) | ISBN 9781668900550 (paperback) |
    ISBN 9781668906316 (ebook) | ISBN 9781668901991 (pdf)
Subjects: LCSH: Hinduism—Juvenile literature. | CYAC: Hinduism—Essence, genius, nature—Juvenile literature.
Classification: LCC BL1203 .B728 2022 | DDC 294.5—dc23
LC record available at https://lccn.loc.gov/2021039874

Printed in the United States of America
Corporate Graphics

ABOUT THE AUTHOR:

Fleur Bradley is originally from the Netherlands. She likes to travel and learn about different cultures whenever she can. Fleur has written many stories for kids and educational books. She now lives in Colorado with her family.

TABLE OF CONTENTS

INTRODUCTION

Religions are systems of faith and worship. Do you practice a religion? About 80 percent of the world's population does. That's 4 out of 5 people.

Every religion is different. Some have one God. That's called **monotheism**. Other religions have multiple gods. This is called **polytheism**. Some religions have an **icon** instead of a god. An icon is an important figure. Hinduism is a polytheistic religion.

Hinduism is the world's third largest religion. About 15 percent of people are Hindu. Most live in India. In the United States, only 1 percent of the population is Hindu. Hinduism is the oldest religion. It is said to be more than 3,000 years old!

Hindus believe in multiple gods. They do not have a single important figure. They believe in a great spirit called **Brahman**. Brahman is the force or spirit present in all things. Hindus believe Brahman can't be seen.

Brahman can be present in many of the Hindu gods. There are many branches of Hinduism. Each branch often has a favorite god.

Hindus practice their faith everywhere. Many homes have small shrines or temples. This is where Hindus pray daily. They wash their hands. Then they offer flowers, fruit, or sweets at the shrine. This worship is called **puja**.

Hindus believe in **reincarnation**. Reincarnation means a person is born again into a new body and life. This cycle of life, death, and rebirth is called samsara. The belief in reincarnation is shared with Buddhism.

Hinduism is often said to be a way of life in India, rather than a religion. The goal of Hindus is to live their lives well. This is called **dharma**. Dharma means duty and virtue. Dharma is lived by worship, doing good work, and not hurting living beings.

Hindus want their soul to be one with Brahman. This goal is called **moksha**. Moksha is considered the highest form of existence.

Doing good in the world is thought to bring good **karma**. Karma means a person's life force.

ॐ MAHATMA GANDHI

Born Mohandas Gandhi in 1869, Gandhi became an important figure to Hindus. He traveled to South Africa and worked to change race laws. Gandhi was known for his nonviolent protests of inequality.

He returned to India in 1915. Gandhi continued his protests against British occupation and oppression. He also worked to unite Muslims and Hindus. Gandhi was called Mahatma for his selfless work. *Mahatma* means "great soul."

Mahatma Gandhi was tragically assassinated in 1948. Assassinate means to kill. His ashes were scattered over the River Ganga. This river in India is thought to be sacred.

Prisha
American Hindu

CHAPTER 1
AN AMERICAN HINDU

The doorbell rings. I run to see who it is. "Good luck and blessings in the New Year," I say as I open the door. It's my friend Becky. She wanted to celebrate **Diwali** with us. She wanted to learn more about my religion. Diwali is the festival of lights. It's my favorite November holiday. I love it even more than Thanksgiving!

Becky hugs me. "I'm so excited, Prisha. Thank you for having me over."

"Of course, but hurry in. It's freezing!" I say, quickly closing the door. Becky is my best friend. She's Jewish and taught me about her religion not too long ago. Now it's my turn.

My little brother, Inesh, peeks his head around the kitchen door. "What are you up to?" he asks. He always wants to join in.

"Prisha is telling me all about Diwali," Becky says before I have a chance to roll my eyes.

Can you find images of Hindu gods? You can search books at the library or the internet. What do they represent? Can you tell by the way they look what purpose they have in the Hindu religion?

Inesh annoys me sometimes, but I decide to be nice. "You can help us make the sweets later," I say. "And put out **diyas**." Diyas are the lanterns for the festival of lights.

"Okay." Inesh grins. "Thank you, Prisha!"

I smile. Maybe this will earn me some good karma. Or at least Mom will be happy.

I help Becky hang up her coat and point upstairs. "Come on. I have stuff set up in my room."

We hurry upstairs and get to work. I show Becky how to use my henna. Henna is a colored powder paste. We draw pretty designs called **mehndi** on our hands.

"Does it come off?" Becky asks.

HINDU GODS

Hinduism has many gods. These are the most popular ones:

Shiva: seen in many forms, sometimes called the Lord of Dance and Time; represents anything from wisdom to fertility

Vishnu: a god of many forms, often depicted as blue and with many arms; wise, majestic, and strong, Vishnu is considered the protector of the universe

Shakti: also called Pervati, goddess of fertility, love, and beauty

"After a week or so," I answer. She draws on my hands. The henna needs to stay on for a while to stain our skin. Then we wash it off.

"Let's go find your brother," Becky says. "I think he's excited about setting up downstairs."

I nod. The truth is, I'm excited too!

Did you know? Many Hindus call their religion "Sanatana Dharma." This means "Eternal Teaching."

CHAPTER 2
A DIWALI CELEBRATION

Inesh is so eager to help us. He almost drops the lanterns!

"Careful," I say, but I can't help but smile. This really is my favorite time of year.

Becky takes a diya and sets it on a side table. "What is Diwali for, exactly?" she asks.

"It's to celebrate the new year, and sometimes the harvest," I say. I set 2 diyas out. I keep half an eye on Inesh.

He sets a diya by the window. His tongue sticks out in concentration. I can't help but laugh.

"Harvest? What harvest?" Becky asks. She looks confused.

"It goes back to ancient farming practices. Indian farmers would celebrate the last harvest of the season. I guess that's where it comes from." I add, "But also, Diwali celebrations invite

Many Hindus chant aum, or om. They do this at the beginning and end of prayers and other rituals. It is thought to be the most sacred word. The sound and symbol are meant to represent gods Brahma, Vishnu, and Shiva.

Lakshmi. Lakshmi is the goddess of good fortune. She likes clean homes. This is why my mom has been cleaning the house—that's the not-so-fun preparation." I make a face.

Becky laughs. "The lanterns are pretty. What else do you do?"

"We make **rangoli**. It's a design we set in the doorway." I show Becky pictures from last year. "We make ours out of flower petals."

Becky nods. "Impressive. I can see why you like Diwali."

I smile and put out the last diya. "Wait until you taste the sweets."

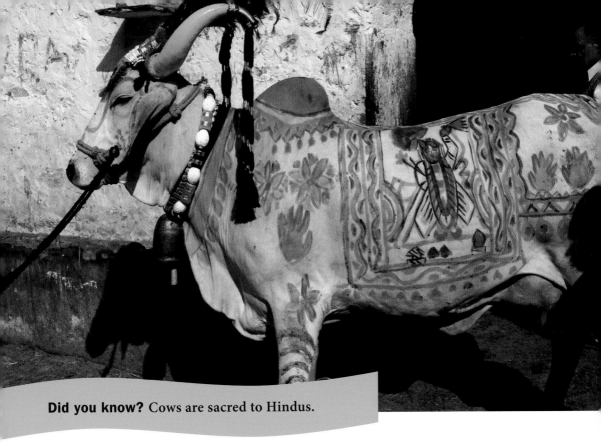

Did you know? Cows are sacred to Hindus.

Just then, my mom gets home. We go help her unpack the groceries in the kitchen.

Mom gives Becky a quick hug. "I'm so glad you're here, Becky."

Inesh jokes, "Mom just wants you to help in the kitchen."

Mom laughs. "We sure can use all the help."

We get to work on making **kheer** first. Kheer is a creamy rice pudding. Then we make **kulfi**. Kulfi is like ice cream.

HOLIDAYS

Hinduism follows a lunar calendar. That means holidays are based on the position of the moon, rather than a specific date. Here are some common Hindu holidays:

Holi: Celebrated late February or early March. Holi is a 2-day festival celebrating spring and various mythological events.

Krishna Janmashtami: Takes place in August or September. This is a 2-day festival celebrating the god Krishna.

Ganesh Chaturthi: An 11-day holiday in August/ September celebrating the birth of god Ganesh.

Navaratri: A 9-day festival celebrated in October to honor goddess Shakti.

Diwali: A 5-day festival in October/November to celebrate light over darkness. It's also a New Year's celebration.

Did you know? Giving offerings is a big part of Hindu worship. Common things to offer a god or goddess are food and flowers!

"Why all the sweets?" Becky asks.

"It's considered an offering for the gods," Mom answers. "And for our guests."

Becky nods. "It's a lot of work. But I'm so happy to join you on Diwali."

I smile. I like sharing my religion. I'm also happy to spend time with my family—right until my little brother drops the bowl of kheer!

I groan. "Inesh!"

Aariv
Indian Hindu

18

CHAPTER 3
A YOUNG HINDU IN INDIA

"Coming at you, Aariv!" my older brother, Darpan, yells. He tackles me in the dirt. We're right outside our house in India.

We wrestle, which helps me calm my nervousness. We're about to go to our **mandir**, or temple. Soon I'll be participating in the Sacred Thread. The Sacred Thread is a special ceremony. It invites people into the Hindu religion. In India, boys between 8 and 12 years old participate.

Darpan already had his Sacred Thread ceremony a few years ago.

"Are you ready for today?" Darpan asks after we sit on the ground.

I brush away some dirt on my clothes. Our mother wouldn't want me to be dirty. The Sacred Thread ceremony is an important **samskara**. That is a Hindu ceremony to mark an important event.

ॐ PATH TO MOKSHA

Moksha is the Hindu goal to be one with Brahman, the force or spirit in all things. There are 4 paths to achieving moksha:

1. Devotion to Brahman

2. Studying and gaining knowledge

3. Being unselfish

4. Meditating and practicing yoga

Meditation means clearing your mind of all thought. Yoga is the practice of exercise to achieve meditation. You have to control your breathing and perform various stretches.

"I'm ready," I say, though I'm not sure. I want to make my family proud.

Mother comes outside, along with our father and my younger twin brothers. There will be more Sacred Thread ceremonies in our family's future!

We walk to the mandir. My mother quickly wipes some dirt off my back. "You boys, always getting messy at the worst times." She smiles and shakes her head.

Inside the mandir, we take off our shoes. Our father takes me to the pandit, or Hindu priest. "Do as you're told," he says firmly, but in a kind voice. He is part of the ceremony.

The priest gives each of us a **bindi**. That's a red mark on our forehead. It's a sign of blessing. The priest then waves a light in front of the shrine. This part of the ceremony is called **arati**.

Cows are considered sacred animals in India. It's often thought to be a superstition, but it's also for practical reasons. Cows are vital to India's agriculture. Are there animals in your culture that are considered sacred? Why?

There are other boys there for the Sacred Thread ceremony as well. I'm second in line. The priest and my father give me a thick cotton thread. There are 3 threads, 1 each for gods Brahma, Vishnu, and Shiva.

I put the thread over my shoulder and tie it at my waist. I will be wearing it until I'm an old man. My hands shake a little, so I clasp them in my lap.

The priest leads prayers in Sanskrit. He says I'm now a twice-born young man. That means I'm ready to start learning from a **guru**. A guru is a spiritual teacher.

I can tell my family is proud. Now, it's time to celebrate!

Prisha and Aariv are both Hindu, but they live in different countries. How is Prisha's experience in the United States different from Aariv's? How is it similar?

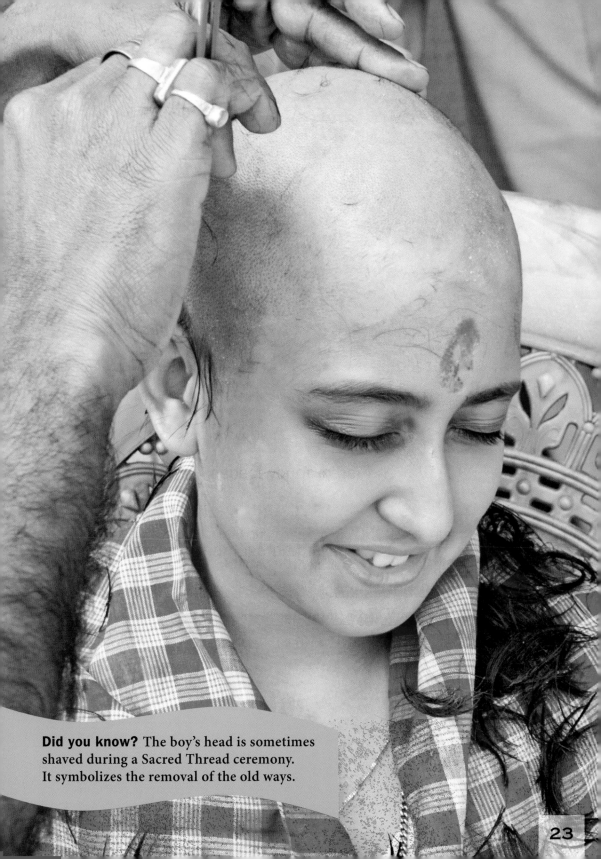

Did you know? The boy's head is sometimes shaved during a Sacred Thread ceremony. It symbolizes the removal of the old ways.

Did you know? The sacred thread used is called "Janoi." It is made up of 3 strands. These strands represent purity in thoughts, words, and actions.

CHAPTER 4
CELEBRATING A SECOND BIRTH

The Sacred Thread ceremony is supposed to be a second birth for boys. I do feel different somehow.

We all celebrate in the town's center, along with other families. There's vegetarian food, enough to feast for a long time. The celebration of the Sacred Thread ceremony will go on for days.

My grandma hands me a plate of food, piled high. "We are so proud of you, Aariv," she says, smiling.

I eat my vegetable curry and rice. The ceremony made me hungry. Hindus are mostly vegetarian in my town. It is so we don't harm a living being, for good karma.

My brother Darpan admires my new threads. "Nice. They'll cut into your skin for a while. But you'll get used to it." He punches me in the arm.

"Be kind to your brother," our mother says in passing. "Tell him about your guru's teachings, Darpan."

Darpan nods his head eagerly. But as soon as our mother leaves, he shakes his head. "I'll have plenty of time to tell you later," he says. Darpan eyes the games going on in the field. "How about some Kabaddi?"

Aariv's Sacred Thread ceremony can be described as a rite of passage. That's something a young person does before being considered a young adult. Can you think of examples of rites of passage in your culture or religion?

ॐ THE FOUR VEDAS

The collections of songs, prayers, and hymns are Hinduism's sacred text. The earliest texts are called the Four Vedas, or Knowledges. They were written in Sanskrit in about 1500 BCE. Sanskrit is an ancient language. Before this, they were passed down as oral traditions. Oral traditions are stories and beliefs people share through speech.

The Four Vedas explain holy rituals and contain stories about the world's creation.

In 700 BCE, the people of the Indus Valley wrote the Upanishads. They are considered the final parts of the Vedas. The Upanishads teach Hindus about the soul (Atman) and truth (Brahman).

Later texts include the Mahabharata and the Ramayana. These long poems tell stories of the Hindu gods and demons.

Did you know? Holi is also the celebration of good winning against evil. It comes from an ancient story about an evil king.

Did you know? Many believe that Buddhism and Sikhism were inspired by the Hindu religion.

Kabaddi is a team game. You have to try to break into the other team's side. And you must tag as many of their players as possible.

"Sure!" I say. It's my favorite game.

Darpan races me to the field. The Sacred Thread ceremony may be about growing up. But I still like to play a few games every once in a while!

ACTIVITY

COOKING KHEER

Prisha cooks kheer, a sweet rice pudding, to celebrate Diwali. Here is a recipe to make your own kheer:

INGREDIENTS:

¼ cup (63 milliliters) of basmati rice

Bowl of water

4 cups (950 mL) of whole milk

½ cup (125 mL) of sugar

¼ teaspoon (1.2 mL) of cardamom powder

Nuts or raisins as desired

DIRECTIONS:

1. Soak the rice for about 30 minutes in a bowl of water.
2. In a saucepan over medium heat, slowly bring the milk to a boil on the stove.
3. Drain the rice. Add the rice to the milk.
4. Cook on low to medium heat until the rice softens.
5. Add sugar and cardamom.
6. Simmer until pudding thickens.
7. Serve with nuts or raisins.

TIMELINE OF MAJOR EVENTS

2500 BCE: The Indus Valley develops a civilization

1500 BCE: The Four Vedas are written

700 BCE: The people of the Indus Valley write the Upanishads

320 BCE: Mauryan Empire starts in India, ending in 400 CE

5 BCE–5 CE: The Mahabharata and the Ramayana are written

October 2, 1869: Gandhi is born

1930: Gandhi was *Time* magazine's Person of the Year

January 30, 1948: Gandhi is killed while at a prayer meeting

2001: A celebration of Maha Kumbh Mela takes place in India in January and February with over 50 million people, the largest gathering on Earth

LEARN MORE

FURTHER READING

Marsico, Katie. *Hinduism*. Ann Arbor, MI: Cherry Lake Publishing, 2017.

Rosinsky, Natalie M. *Hinduism*. Mankato, MN: Compass Point Books, 2010.

Self, David. *The Lion Encyclopedia of World Religions*. Oxford, U.K.: Lion Children's, 2008.

WEBSITES

Britannica Kids—Hinduism
https://kids.britannica.com/kids/article/Hinduism/353249

Primary Homework Help—Hinduism
http://www.primaryhomeworkhelp.co.uk/religion/hinduism.htm

GLOSSARY

arati (uh-RAH-tee) a ceremonial movement of light in front of icons

bindi (BIN-dee) a small dot on forehead placed by a Hindu priest as a sign of blessing

Brahman (BRAH-muhn) the force or spirit present in all things

dharma (DAR-muh) the Hindu goal to live a good life

Diwali (dih-WAH-lee) festival of lights that ushers in the New Year

diyas (DEE-yuhs) the lanterns used during Diwali

guru (GUHR-ooh) a spiritual teacher

icon (EYE-kahn) an important figure

karma (KAR-muh) the good or bad forces created by person's acts in life

kheer (KEER) a sweet rice pudding

kulfi (KUHL-fee) a sweet dish, like ice cream

mandir (MUHN-dir) a Hindu temple

mehndi (MEN-dee) intricate designs often painted in henna

moksha (MOHK-shuh) goal of Hindus to achieve enough good karma to reach salvation of the cycle of rebirth

monotheism (mah-nuh-THEE-ih-zuhm) the belief in one God

polytheism (PAH-lee-thee-ih-zuhm) the belief in multiple gods

puja (POO-juh) worship, either at home or in a temple

rangoli (rahn-GOH-lee) designs made out of flowers or chalk powder; often used during Diwali to welcome gods

reincarnation (ree-in-kar-NAY-shuhn) the rebirth of a person's soul into another being after death

samskara (samz-KAH-ruh) a Hindu ceremony for an important event

INDEX